HILARY WILSON

EGYPTIAN FOOD
AND DRINK

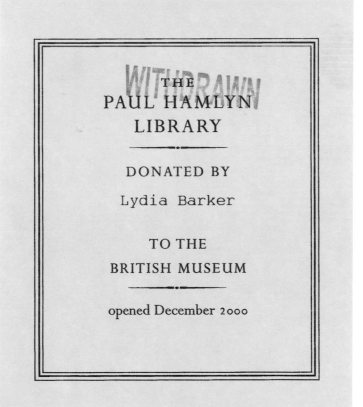

SHIRE EGYPTOLOGY

2

Cover illustration
The king offers food to the gods.
(Author's painting after a relief in the temple of Seti I at Abydos.)

British Library Cataloguing in Publication Data.
Wilson, Hilary.
Egyptian food and drink.
1. Ancient Egypt. Food. Cultural aspects.
I. Title.
641. 3'00932.
ISBN 0-85263-972-4

Published by
SHIRE PUBLICATIONS LTD
Cromwell House, Church Street, Princes Risborough,
Aylesbury, Bucks HP17 9AJ, UK.

Series Editor: Barbara Adams

ISBN 0 85263 972 4

First published 1988

Set in 11 point Times and printed in Great Britain by
C. I. Thomas & Sons (Haverfordwest) Ltd.
Press Buildings, Merlins Bridge, Haverfordwest, Dyfed.

Contents

Acknowledgements

Several people have helped and encouraged me in preparing this book. In particular I would like to thank T. G. H. James of the British Museum, Laura Ponsonby of the Royal Botanic Gardens, Kew, and Professor D. L. Hawksworth of the Commonwealth Mycological Institute, Kew. Thanks also to Geoffrey Cooper and Robin Thomas for help with photography. Where Herodotus is quoted, the translation used is the 1968 Penguin edition. Quotations from Egyptian sources have been adapted from collections of Egyptian literature by Adolf Erman and Miriam Lichtheim. Line drawings have been taken from photographs or original monuments except where stated. Finally, my very special thanks to my husband, Philip, who made it possible for me to visit Egypt for the first time, and to my children, Richard, Thomas, Jenny and Hugh, who have put up with much in the name of research.

4

List of illustrations

Chronology

From W. J. Murnane, *The Penguin Guide to Ancient Egypt*, 1983.

Predynastic	before 3050 BC		
Early Dynastic	3050-2686 BC		
		3050-2890	*Dynasty 1*
			Aha
		2890-2686	*Dynasty II*
		2686-2613	*Dynasty III*
			Djoser
Old Kingdom	2613-2181 BC		
		2613-2498	*Dynasty IV*
		2498-2345	*Dynasty V*
		2491-2477	Sahure
		2453-2422	Niuserre
		2375-2345	Unas
		2345-2181	*Dynasty VI*
First Intermediate Period	2181-2040 BC		
		2181-2040	*Dynasties VII to X*
Middle Kingdom	2040-1782 BC		
		2060-1991	*Dynasty XI*
		1991-1782	*Dynasty XII*
		1991-1962	Amenemhat I
		1971-1928	Sesostris I
Second Intermediate Period	1782-1570 BC		
		1782-1570	*Dynasties XIII-XVII*
New Kingdom	1570-1070 BC		
		1570-1293	*Dynasty XVIII*
		1551-1524	Amenophis I
		1524-1518	Tuthmosis I
		1504-1450	Tuthmosis III
		1498-1483	Hatshepsut
		1386-1349	Amenophis III
		1350-1334	Amenophis IV/ Akhenaten
		1334-1325	Tutankhamun
		1293-1185	*Dynasty XIX*
		1291-1278	Seti I
		1279-1212	Ramesses II
		1185-1070	*Dynasty XX*
		1182-1151	Ramesses III
Third Intermediate Period	1070-713 BC		
		1070-713	*Dynasties XXI-XXIV*
Late Period	713-332 BC		
		713-525	*Dynasties XXV-XXVI (Nubian)*
		525-343	*Dynasties XXVII-XXX (Persian)*
Graeco-Roman Period	332 BC-AD 395		Ptolemies and Roman Emperors

1. Relief from the Third Dynasty tomb of Rahotep at Meydum. Funerary offerings are tabulated on the right and listed in abbreviated form around the offering table. (BM 1242, author's photograph. Courtesy of the Trustees of the British Museum.)

2. Hieroglyph for 'offerings of bread and beer'.

3. A gardener carries water from the river to the area of square garden plots shown to the right. Relief from Amarna. (Brooklyn Museum 65.16. Charles Edwin Wilbour Fund. Reproduced by courtesy of the Brooklyn Museum.)

1
Introduction

Food features prominently in Egyptian wall paintings and reliefs of all periods. Old Kingdom tomb owners are shown overseeing the work of their servants preparing and delivering all manner of foodstuffs, Middle Kingdom tomb models reproduce the activities of the bakery, brewery and butcher's yard and New Kingdom monarchs are portrayed offering to the gods plates of bread, meat and vegetables.

Food was naturally essential to the Egyptians but Eighteenth Dynasty paintings of dinner parties show that the affluent upper class enjoyed the luxury of eating for pleasure. Fasting, or at least abstaining from certain foods, was a recognised sign of respect for the dead during the period preceding the burial. The family of the deceased would break their fast by partaking in a funeral banquet.

Many tomb paintings showing food production and preparation were intended to ensure a plentiful supply for the deceased in the netherworld. The better-off Egyptian spent much of his life preparing for death, hoping to provide for eternity everything he had enjoyed in his mortal existence. On his funerary stela he might propound his titles and lineage and enumerate his family but primarily he would pray for the continuance of food offerings. The simplest offerings, represented by the hieroglyph for oblations, were bread and beer. Space permitting, commodities such as meat, fowl, fruit, vegetables, oils and unguents would also be requested, but bread and beer were the staples of the Egyptian diet, whatever a man's status.

Evidence from non-funerary contexts as to methods of preparing and cooking food is sparse. There are few settlement sites available for archaeological investigation since most major sites are still areas of occupation, especially in the Delta, which was the agricultural heartland of ancient Egypt. Those domestic sites which have been excavated are not necessarily typical. The village of the Twelfth Dynasty pyramid-builders at Kahun in the Fayum and the New Kingdom village of the royal tomb-builders at Deir el-Medina were separate from other settlements and had a different social structure. The town areas of Amarna, built by Akhenaten in the Eighteenth Dynasty, were occupied for barely twenty years.

Horticulture leaves little archaeological evidence and garden plots were too prosaic to warrant much space on tomb walls. Preferred scenes were grain fields, groves of fruit trees and vineyards. Changes in climate and ecology within the last 4000 years must be considered. Plants which once grew wild in Egypt are no longer found there.

4. Collection of funerary food offerings including portions of duck, loaves of bread and dishes of figs and dried fish. (BM 35939, reproduced by courtesy of the Trustees of the British Museum.)
5. Hieroglyph for 'taste', 'smell' and 'enjoy'.

Others, stylised in paintings and hieroglyphs, are unidentifiable. Similarly, animals and birds which once thrived in the Nile Valley have not done so for centuries. Crops now associated with Egypt, such as cotton, sugar cane and potatoes, are modern introductions.

No Egyptian culinary recipe books are known, although papyri listing medicinal concoctions indicate ways in which foodstuffs could have been prepared. The contributions of such classical commentators as Herodotus, though not always reliable, are still valuable. Their observations refer to later periods of Egyptian history, by which time Greek fashions had been introduced into upper-class households and food items were imported to suit Hellenistic palates.

Late New Kingdom documents like the Papyri Anastasi, which include lists of foods consumed by Ramesses III during a royal progress, and the Great Harris Papyrus, which itemises offerings at major temples during his reign, are rare and their details tantalisingly incomplete. Such linguistic nuances as the differences between types of loaf are impossible to resolve. By modern analogy, the precise differentiation between buns, baps and barmcakes would be difficult to explain.

Food remains from tombs are of great interest, many specimens having survived in an immediately recognisable form. Beer and wine stored in semi-porous jars evaporate quickly and their residues are not easily analysed. Fats, oils and dairy produce degenerate to an unappetising collection of basic organic chemicals. The Egyptians' habit of labelling food containers helps to create lists of the edible products considered fit for inclusion in the tomb even though the contents have disintegrated.

The Egyptians considered smell and taste to be important senses. Guests at Nebamun's dinner-party during the reign of Amenophis III are shown holding lotus blooms to their noses and wearing cones of perfumed wax on their wigs. Incense burning was an essential part of temple ritual. The 'nose' hieroglyph was a determinative for 'smell' and 'taste', but also for 'enjoy' and 'take pleasure in'. The Egyptians clearly considered eating a sensual experience as well as being an essential aspect of everyday life.

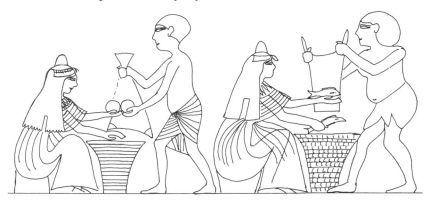

6. Market scene. Grain in small sacks is offered in exchange for fish and round objects which might be fishcakes, cheeses or small loaves. Theban tomb of Ipuy, Nineteenth Dynasty. (After Davies.)

7. Triangular loaf of bread. (BM 40942, reproduced by courtesy of the Trustees of the British Museum.)

8. Baking and brewing. Relief from the tomb chapel of Hetepherakht. (Reproduced by courtesy of the Rijksmuseum van Oudheden, Leiden.)

2
Bread and beer

It is not certain whether wheat or barley was the most ancient cultivated grain in Egypt. In earliest times there was no distinction made between them, both being called simply 'grain' or 'seeds'. Barley (*Hordeum vulgare*) has been found at prehistoric sites like Merimda in the Delta, dating from before 4000 BC. The main variety of wheat grown in Egypt was emmer (*Triticum dicoccum*). Both grains are generally termed 'corn', as when Jacob told his sons: 'I have heard there is corn in Egypt' (Genesis 42:2).

The amount of land available for cultivation allowed Egypt to export large quantities of grain, particularly to Rome in the latest periods. The Fayum was always a prime cereal-growing area, the waters of Lake Moeris being used for irrigation. Several Twelfth Dynasty pharaohs reclaimed land there for agriculture, lowering the level of the lake and extending the fertile margin. During the Ptolemaic period, the Fayum was the most prosperous and densely populated region of Egypt.

Grain was a staple food and so important in the diet that it constituted a major item in the food rations paid as wages to royal workmen. Market scenes from tombs show bags of grain being bartered for all manner of goods. Corn was a taxable commodity. Each year, assessors measured the fields and sampled the grain to estimate the yield. A tax demand would then be issued and at harvest time the tax collectors returned to record the value of the grain garnered and to see that the tax due was delivered to the state or temple granaries.

It is not clear in what proportions barley and wheat were grown. Both were used for bread and barley also for beer. Loaves included as grave goods have proved to be predominantly of wheat flour, probably because it produced a fine bread considered most suitable for funerary offerings. Almost certainly, barley bread was more common in poorer households than that made from emmer.

Small loaves of barley bread were included in the funerary banquet found by Emery in the Second Dynasty tomb (3477) at Saqqara. This gourmet meal (which will be referred to again as the Saqqara banquet) was prepared for a noblewoman and had been set out beside the burial pit within her mastaba. It is highly unlikely that such an elaborate meal would have been provided often, even for the highest nobility, and it must be seen as a special case. However, it gives valuable information about the kinds of food enjoyed by the

Egyptian Food and Drink

9. Sieve for cribbling crushed grain. The extraction of flour using such sieves cannot have been higher than 80 per cent. (BM 55130, reproduced by courtesy of the Trustees of the British Museum.)

Egyptians, even at this early period, and the ways in which they were prepared and presented.

Grain was sown by hand and trodden into the soil by animals, usually sheep or goats. At harvest time, the stems were cut just below the ears and the straw was left to be collected for such purposes as brick-making, animal bedding and fodder or domestic fuel. The harvest was carried in baskets to the threshing floor where sheep, cattle or donkeys were driven around, trampling it to separate the grain from the husks. Winnowers tied cloths around their heads to protect them from the dust. They threw the corn into the air from wooden scoops and the wind blew away the chaff while the heavier grain fell back to earth.

There were many uses for barley and wheat. Whole grain could be cooked to accompany meat or vegetables or to thicken soup or gruel. Crushed grain was used to make a sort of porridge, as included in the Saqqara banquet. Rough cakes like flapjacks or oatcakes could be made by mixing crushed grain with oil or animal fat, but by far the most important cereal product was bread.

Reliefs, models and paintings of all periods show that flour was milled daily in quantity in Egyptian households. First the grain was crushed in a limestone mortar set into the floor. Then it was milled on a sloping stone, known by its dished shape as a saddle quern, by means of a rubbing stone (see figure 8, top). The rotary quern was not introduced into Egypt until the Graeco-Roman period. Quern emplacements have been found at Kahun, the Twelfth Dynasty village of the pyramid-builders, and in the workmen's village at Amarna, serving the city built by Akhenaten in the Eighteenth Dynasty (see figure 65).

The unusual degree of wear on the teeth of Egyptian mummies is thought to be due to large amounts of mineral impurities present in ancient bread, which was the staple food of all classes. Such contamination could come from wind-blown sand at any stage of harvesting, storage or milling. It is also thought to come from certain types of stone used for querns. At Amarna, the 1986-7 Egypt Exploration Society team under Barry Kemp carried out experiments into the various stages of bread preparation. The flour they produced on a saddle quern was found to be freer of sand and grit than had been expected.

Once the grain had been ground it was passed through rushwork sieves. These were inefficient and the flour obtained was coarse and contained amounts of whole or partly crushed grain. To promote a better extraction of flour, the grain was often parched, that is, soaked to soften the tough outer layers and then dried on mats in the sun before milling.

The basic flat loaf resembling pitta bread, which is still the commonest type of bread in Egypt, was made in much the same way as today. Flour was mixed with water and a little salt in a large container shaped like a pancheon, the Arabic *magur*. Unleavened dough could be shaped by hand and cooked directly on a flat stone placed over the fire, on the baking floor inside a clay oven, or even by be-

10. Bakers in the kitchen of Ramesses III. Round loaves are cooked on the outside of the cylindrical oven, which has flames emerging from its open top. (After Rosellini.)

11. Seti I offers food to Osiris. Included are loaves with central depressions and slashes, wedge-shaped honey cakes, fruit, ducks and flowers. (The Metropolitan Museum of Art. Gift of J. Pierpont Morgan, 1911. Reproduced by courtesy of the Metropolitan Museum of Art.)

ing slapped on to the pottery wall of the oven itself. Some loaves were simply cooked in the ashes of the fire.

Leavening was most probably effected by the method current in Egyptian villages. The *magur* is washed around with water to remove the dough sticking to it from the previous batch. More flour is added and mixed to a paste which is left overnight to sour. The sour dough starter then forms the basis of the next day's bread mix. Bread has been leavened in this way in Egypt for thousands of years, but more sophisticated means of leavening were also available. Analyses of bread and beer samples have proved that the Egyptians were using a pure form of yeast at least as early as 1500 BC. This organism (*Saccharomyces winlocki*) was probably obtained in liquid barm form from the brewery, which was usually closely associated with the bakery.

Some modern writers, such as Schweinfurth and Wresinski, quote the use of lichens in the making of bread in Egypt. It is true that lichens are included in some Islamic meat dishes, for which purpose they are imported from great distances. Only two lichens are attested from the Dynastic age by specimens found in a Twenty-first Dynasty funerary cache at Deir el-Bahri, but these were of European, probably Greek, origin. No lichens of the sort suitable for cooking grow in Egypt. The nearest sources of such lichens are the mountains of Morocco and part of the higher Ethiopian plateau.

The lichen *Evernia furfuracea* was probably imported for use in perfumery and as packing material for mummies. Although the addition of lichens might improve the porosity of bread and its keeping qualities and deter attack by insects or fungi, it is improbable that the Egyptians would have gone to the trouble of importing them from Greece in the quantities required for such a basic, everyday activity as bread-making. The use of Iceland moss as a leavening agent was suggested by Wresinski, but this is even more unlikely, for two reasons. Lichens have no known leavening properties and the nearest sources of Iceland moss are Scandinavia and the Russian tundra.

Some loaves were shaped with a central cavity or depression which may have been used for a garnish such as a portion of beans or an egg, as is sometimes the case with modern *eish shami*. Some of the cavities are off-centre and too small to have served this purpose. They would appear to be the marks of the stick with which the loaf was pushed into the oven or removed from it, as shown in the bakery scene from the late New Kingdom tomb of Ramesses III. A com-

12. Scenes in the kitchens of Ramesses III. (Top) A fire is fuelled beneath a stew pot. (Bottom) Pastrycooks make fancy-shaped cakes and loaves. (After Rosellini.)

mon shape for loaves was semicircular, from which derived the hieroglyph for the letter T, the word for bread itself being *ta*. Loaves of this shape were included in the Eighteenth Dynasty tomb of Tutankhamun.

Loaves were shaped in ovals, triangles and indented squares, all of which appear among offerings. Some are shown with slashes across the crust, which enabled the bread to rise evenly. Some loaves were modelled in the form of animals, human figures or fancy shapes popular for special occasions such as religious festivals. Some were probably sweetened and flavoured with nuts or spices.

Bread was also baked in moulds, the most common shape being conical. Such loaves, halved, are often shown stacked on a table before a tomb owner. The pots, made of Nile silt moulded over a wooden core, were usually broken to extract the loaves. The central area of Amarna is littered with sherds of bread moulds which were produced in thousands at the bakery attached to the great temple. Experiments in making and using these moulds have produced perfectly edible loaves of the sort which the Egyptians called 'festival bread'.

Several tomb models and pictures show stacks of wider, shallower moulds being heated over a fire (see figure 49). It is possible that the pre-heated pot speeded up the baking of a loaf or the formation of a firm crust, but it is also possible that these scenes show the tempering of the pots. Tempering in a baking context means greasing the inside of a pot, heating it to baking temperature and repeating the process several times to create a temporary non-stick surface. Many pot-baked loaves have been found with complete crusts, showing that not all stuck in their moulds. Moulds were also made with raised designs on the inner surface to give a fancy pattern to the loaf. As these moulds had been used several times, it seems that the bread

13. The palace kitchens at Amarna. (Far left) Round loaves are prepared on a stove; (left of centre) conical bread moulds are buried in embers. (The Brooklyn Museum. Charles Edwin Wilbour Fund. Reproduced by courtesy of the Brooklyn Museum.)

Bread and beer   17

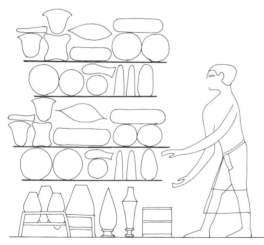

14. Bakers in the 'cake room' prepare a purée or jam of dates and honey to serve with triangular *shat* loaves. Theban tomb of Rekhmire, Eighteenth Dynasty. (After Davies.)

15. Shelves in the bakery laden with a variety of shapes of loaves and cakes. Beer jars stand in racks beneath. Theban tomb of Rekhmire, Eighteenth Dynasty. (After Davies.)

was removed from the pot without too much difficulty.

Sometimes the baking pot was covered with a lid before being placed in the oven. This would have produced a softer bread, cooked in steam which could not escape so easily from the covered mould. Some moulded bread was coated with seeds like cumin, which could be shaken around the greased mould before the dough was added (see figure 56).

Dough was also enriched with fat, milk or eggs, or sweetened with honey or fruit. A fruit loaf in the Dokki Agriculture Museum in Cairo was made by layering mashed dates between two discs of dough. Stacks of brown triangular slices among offerings are thought to repre-

16. Tomb model showing brewing, baking and butchery. (Left) A cylinder oven, a domed bake-oven and a saddle quern; (middle) water carrier, beer jar, and barley mash being sieved; (right) trussed ox and butcher with knife. (BM 41576, reproduced by courtesy of the Trustees of the British Museum.)

sent honey cakes, a popular luxury. Other fancy cakes or pastries were made in the 'cake room'. Pastrycooks were called 'workers in dates' because dates were the commonest sweetener available.

Hieroglyphic terms for over thirty types of bread, cake and biscuit are known but it is impossible positively to identify many of these terms with particular recipes. There were breads made with *nabk* berries and the flesh of the *dom* palm nut but it is unclear how they were made or whether the fruit was mixed with flour or other ingredients. The bakery scene in the tomb of Rekhmire (Eighteenth Dynasty) shows most of the stages in the preparation of a loaf or cake called *shat,* a highly valued temple offering. The distinctive ingredient was ground tigernuts and the triangular loaves were sweetened with honey and dates. In the same tomb is shown an array of baked goods, loaves and cakes in a variety of shapes, all labelled but sadly without accompanying recipes or descriptions.

Another product of the bakery was the lightly cooked bread made from coarsely ground barley, which was used in beer-making. Beer was the drink of the people and the basic liquid requirement in funerary offerings. Its strength was denoted by colour, red being popular and black the strongest brew. It was prepared in quantity in all households and the rich could afford to import Syrian and Nubian beers.

The process of beer-making was much the same as that used to prepare Sudanese *bouza*. Thick, leavened loaves were partly baked so as not to destroy the enzymes which promote fermentation. The loaves were crumbled, mixed with water and perhaps some crushed, malted grain and the mash was allowed to ferment through the action of the yeast and the warm climate. The resultant thick, soup-like concoction was strained through a sieve into a large vat from which it was decanted into smaller jars (see figure 8, bottom).

Vegetable or fruit products were sometimes added to flavour or give body to the beer, the most commonly quoted being dates, but hops were unknown to the Egyptians. In the fifth century BC Herodotus mentioned the Egyptians' 'wine' prepared from barley and claimed they had no vines. He was undoubtedly recording his own observation that beer was the commonest alcoholic drink made in Egypt. Diodorus, writing in the first century BC, claimed that, for taste and smell, Egyptian beer was not much inferior to wine.

The Egyptians considered it one of life's pleasures to get drunk and at the annual festival of the goddess Hathor at Dendera vast quantities of beer were handed out to pilgrims. There were, nevertheless, problems associated with drinking to excess. In a passage from a Nineteenth Dynasty schoolboy manuscript, the student scribe is warned against the evils of beer: 'I am told . . . you go from street to street where everything stinks to high heaven of beer. Beer will turn men away from you and send your soul to perdition. You are like a broken rudder on a ship . . . like a shrine without its god, like a house without bread.'

Cereal products were at the heart of Egyptian society, forming the basis of the economy and the bulk of the national diet. A house without bread was, therefore, a sad and mean place.

19. (Above) An Amarnan workman eats his basket lunch of bread, cucumber and onion. From the reconstructed wall of the Aten temple at Karnak, now in the Luxor Museum.

17. (Above) Gardener lifting water by means of a *shaduf* from the garden pond. The plants include a pomegranate tree, mandrake and lotus. Nineteenth Dynasty tomb at Thebes.

18. Garden plots excavated during the 1986 season of the Egypt Exploration Society's work at Amarna. (By courtesy of the Committee of the Egypt Exploration Society.)

3
All growing things

Egyptian gardening scenes are very rare. Ornamental gardens shown in some New Kingdom tombs record the Egyptians' love for shady trees and perfumed flowers but kitchen gardens supplying household vegetables are not seen. The physical and pictorial records give a good idea of what vegetables were grown but not how they were grown.

The major part of Egypt's arable land was given over to cereals and flax and these are the crops usually featured in agricultural scenes. As in modern Egypt, small plots of domestic crops would have been cultivated between the larger fields. Irrigation systems gave the land a chequerboard appearance, each 'field' divided into squares by low ridges of earth enabling small areas to be watered individually. The water was lifted from irrigation ditches by hand or by a *shaduf,* which was introduced during the New Kingdom and is still used in arable areas of Egypt. Water was poured directly on to the land or into storage tanks and caring for the garden was a strenuous job, as indicated by this extract from the late Old Kingdom text, the *Instruction of Duauf*: 'The gardener brings loads and his arms and neck ache beneath them. In the morning he waters the vegetables, and at evening the vines.'

Garden plots took the form of small beds made by surrounding an area with low mud-brick walls and filling the enclosure with soil, sometimes over a layer of sand. Such garden plots have been identified at the workmen's village at Amarna, built in an area of desert land most inhospitable to plant life. Despite the provision of food supplies by the state, the villagers still felt the need to grow their own vegetables.

The Egyptian workman's packed lunch consisted of bread, beer and onions. Herodotus was told that quantities of onions and radishes were given as wages to the builders of Khufu's pyramid. Bunches of onions with green stems and round, white bulbs are shown draped over offering tables. In the Pyramid Texts of the late Old Kingdom, onions are likened to sound white teeth. The small ancient onions were probably sweeter and less eye-watering than their modern equivalent.

Garlic was grown from earliest times, clay models of garlic bulbs having been found in Predynastic burials at Naqada. A bunch of garlic bulbs, with their stems bound in the same way as onions, was found in the Eighteenth Dynasty tomb of Kha, the architect to Amenophis

20. Lettuces presented as offerings to Min at Luxor. (Photograph by C. F. Lock about 1912, from a negative in the possession of Robin Thomas.)

21. Faience models of cucumbers, an onion and a stylised bunch of grapes. From a Twelfth Dynasty tomb at Lisht. (Metropolitan Museum of Art Excavations, 1923-4. By courtesy of the Metropolitan Museum of Art.)

III. The ancient kind was smaller than the modern cultivated species, had as many as 45 cloves to each bulb and was probably milder in flavour.

Lettuces, although included among food offerings, are not immediately recognisable. The shape is elongated like a Cos lettuce. They were considered particularly suitable offerings to Min, the god of agriculture, procreation and fertility. At Luxor the king is shown offering lettuces to the ithyphallic god. In medical papyri, lettuce is recommended as a cure for impotence and is traditionally held to have aphrodisiac properties.

Some of the green bundles usually interpreted as lettuce (see figure 22) may be *meloukhia* (*Corchorus olitorius*). This member of the hemp family is extremely popular today throughout the Middle East and the ancient plant name *shemshemet* may possibly be identified with *meloukhia*. The young, deep green leaf shoots are picked like spinach and may be eaten fresh or dried for winter storage. *Meloukhia* has a bitter flavour, like endive, and is used as a base for many dishes. The glutinous quality of the leaves will thicken a simple stock to produce a soup which is a traditional Egyptian peasant dish, considered to be a legacy from the pharaohs. Peasant women take large pots of *meloukhia* into the fields as a midday meal for their menfolk.

Despite Herodotus' statement, radishes are not shown among offerings. Seeds, some displayed at the Dokki Agriculture Museum in Cairo, have been found in quantities dating from Dynastic times. The type grown bore little resemblance to the modern salad variety, having elongated and thickened roots, often white or pink rather than red. Radishes were probably cooked like turnips.

There is little physical evidence for the cultivation of leeks in ancient Egypt but they are mentioned often in literature and the Egyptian word for leeks was used for vegetables in general. The Hebrews, wandering in the wilderness after the Exodus, complained about their boring diet of manna and quails, remembering fondly the range of fresh food they had enjoyed in Egypt: 'Think of it! In Egypt we had fish for the asking, cucumbers and water-melons, leeks and onions and garlic' (Numbers 11:5).

The cucumbers mentioned were of the same type to be found today in every market in Egypt. They are small, blunt-ended, have fewer seeds than the European ridge variety and a less bitter taste. Cucumbers of this description, with curled-over stalks, often fill the gaps between other food offerings. Wooden and faience models of cucumbers were included in many burials. Small cucumbers could have been pickled to provide a year-round supply of vegetables. Pickles still form an important part of the Egyptian breakfast or *mezze*

22. Stela of Sensebek, Twelfth Dynasty. Offerings include meat, bread, onions, grapes, cucumber or melon and lettuce. (BM 580, author's photograph. By courtesy of the Trustees of the British Museum.)

menu.

Some large, green objects on offering tables could be melons or marrows and several types are still grown in Egypt. Seeds from melons, particularly the pink-fleshed water-melon known as *bedoukhia* to the ancients, have been found in many sites, including Amarna. Marrow or courgettes are almost indistinguishable in size, colour and shape from green melons and cucumbers, and their seeds are also very similar.

Interestingly, Herodotus claimed that the Egyptians hated beans: '. . . as for beans, they cannot even bear to look at them, because they imagine they are unclean (in point of fact the Egyptians never sow beans, and even if any happen to grow wild, they will not eat them, either raw or boiled).'

However, from very ancient times beans, peas and lentils have been included in Egyptian tombs and many are exhibited at Dokki. The most easily recognisable type is the chick-pea, white and knobbly with a little 'beak', which explains why the Egyptians called it 'hawk face'. They could have been served as a vegetable or ground into flour used to enrich bread dough. The most popular modern chick-pea recipe from the Middle East is *hummus,* a spread or pâté made from mashed chick-peas and sesame oil. Chick-pea sellers roam Egyptian markets in late summer selling cones of salted chick-peas with a squeeze of lemon juice.

Earlier in the year, lupine (*Lupinus digitatus*), called *tirmiss* in Arabic, is sold in the markets. Examples of lupine, and several other types of pulse, have been found at Abusir in the Fifth Dynasty suntemple of Sahure. Lupine seeds are like flat, yellow broad beans. They have a very bitter taste when raw and have to be boiled then soaked in many changes of water over several days to make them palatable. They are, nevertheless, a popular snack delicacy, being eaten by biting the seed to press the flesh into the mouth and then discarding the skin.

Another type of bean identified from ancient sources is *ful nabed,* a pale variety of the common broad bean (*Vicia faba*). Pharaonic cooks almost certainly invented *ta'amia* or *felafel,* fried rissoles made from mashed beans, onion, garlic and spices. Coptic Christians consume large quantities of *felafel* during Lent. The Copts are said to be descended from the ancient Egyptians and many of their traditions are so old that their origins may well lie in Dynastic times.

The smaller brown beans known as *ful medames* (*metmes* in Coptic) are the basis of the classic national Egyptian dish of the same name. There is a modern Egyptian saying that 'Beans have satisfied even the pharaohs' and the simple dish of *ful* is thought to have a very long pedigree. Beans are stewed with oil, garlic, fresh herbs and spices and served with plain bread. The dish is often cooked overnight in an earthenware pot in the ashes of the day's fire. Hard-boiled eggs, dried fish and pickles are served as accompaniments.

Lentils were being cultivated before 3150 BC, as shown from analysis of the stomach contents of Predynastic bodies. Stores of several varieties of beans and lentils were found in the subterranean galleries of the Third Dynasty Step Pyramid at Saqqara. Faience models of speckled *lubia* beans and black-eyed beans have been found dating from the Fifth Dynasty. Yellow peas have been found in abundance at the Twelfth Dynasty pyramid sites of Hawara and Kahun, showing that they were extensively cultivated at least as early as the Middle Kingdom. Lentils were among the goods used by the Egyptians to barter for cedarwood in the Lebanon, as recorded in the Late Period story of the 'Voyage of Wenamun'. Other identified pulses grown in ancient Egypt include cow peas, pigeon peas, asparagus beans and grass peas.

Besides vegetables grown in gardens and field plots there were food plants to be harvested from the wild. The multi-purpose papyrus plant (*Cyperus papyrus*) is mentioned by Herodotus as being eaten in this way: 'They pull up the annual crop of papyrus-reed which grows in the marshes, cut the stalks in two and eat the lower part . . . first baking it in a closed pan, heated red-hot, if they want to enjoy it to perfection.' The young shoots of papyrus could also have been eaten like bamboo shoots.

The most popular of ancient Egyptian flowers, the so-called lotus, was also a source of food. There were two sorts of lotus or water-lily mentioned by Herodotus, the white (*Nymphaea lotus*) being known from the Old Kingdom and used in festival garlands, bouquets and offerings. Its name in Egyptian was *seshen,* which has survived through Coptic and Arabic as the name Susan. The black-skinned lily root, 'the size of an apple', according to Herodotus, was peeled and the inner white part eaten either raw, baked or boiled.

The pink lotus (*Nelumbium speciosum*) produces a seed head 'shaped like a wasp's comb'. Each contains up to 36 seeds the size of an olive stone, which are sometimes called Egyptian beans. These and the roots of the lily were eaten in ancient times. Models of the seed heads made of clay and faience have been found but none dates from earlier than the Eighteenth Dynasty, when the pink lotus was introduced into Egypt.

Vegetables of all sorts formed a large and important part of the Egyptian diet and, together with bread, formed the basis of most meals. It is likely that most Egyptian peasants existed on a purely vegetarian diet, only dreaming of meat and relishing the occasional luxury of fish or wildfowl.

23. Plants of papyrus (left) and lotus (centre) as depicted by an ancient Egyptian artist.
24. (Right) The Egyptian lotus (*Nelumbium speciosum*). (After Maspero.)

4
Wine and fruit of all kinds

Among ancient Egyptian food plants, fruit trees were very important. The most significant was the sycamore fig (*Ficus sycomorus*), also known as the wild fig. The leaves, unlike the lobed leaves of the true fig (*Ficus carica*), are oval. The fruits grow in twos and threes from separate stalks, while true figs grow singly from leaf nodes on the main stem. Sycamore figs are smaller, yellower and have a more astringent taste than ordinary figs but were a most popular dessert fruit from very early times. The dish of stewed fruit in the Second Dynasty Saqqara banquet described as being 'possibly figs' is more likely to be sycamore figs as these were far more common and enjoyed by all strata of society. The tree was held sacred to the goddess Hathor, who was known as 'Lady of the Sycamore'.

The true fig seems to have been introduced into Egypt before the Old Kingdom. Two examples of schist dishes shaped like fig leaves were found by Emery in the Archaic Period necropolis at Saqqara. The trees were smaller and more bush-like than sycamore figs and probably confined to the gardens of the wealthy. The fig harvest was an event considered important enough to be portrayed in tombs. Gardeners are shown competing for the fruit with monkeys which may have been household pets. Besides being grown for eating, figs were used to make a wine and a liqueur which was likened to flame because of the way it burned the throat.

A tree of equal importance with the fig was the date palm. Coloured representations of palms laden with fruit show that the predominant species in ancient times bore yellow or brown dates. Finds of date stones have been made at numerous sites from the Predynastic era onwards. Apart from being eaten fresh or dried, dates were made into a purée or jam to accompany festival bread and are thought to have been used to enrich and flavour beer. A wine was made from dates and a sort of toddy could be made from the sap of the palm but, as this was destructive of the trees, it cannot have been a common practice.

The earliest evidence of the vine in Egypt comes from the Predynastic settlement of El Omari south of Cairo, where wild vine seeds have been found. Many finds of grapes or sun-dried raisins, often indistinguishable, have been made in tombs of all ages, and bunches of blue-black grapes and baskets of similar coloured fruit are common in offering scenes. Dessert grapes were included *c.* 1325 BC in an attractive bottle-shaped basket in Tutankhamun's burial.

Egyptian Food and Drink

25. Birds in a fig tree (detail). The oval leaves identify *Ficus sycomorus*. Theban tomb of Nakht, Eighteenth Dynasty.

26. Fig harvest with baboons. The lobed leaves identify *Ficus carica*. Tomb of Khnum-hotpe at Beni Hasan, Twelfth Dynasty. (After Davies.)

An alabaster jar from the same tomb was found to contain a sugary residue identified as the remains of grape juice rather than fermented wine.

The special attention lavished on vines, particularly the copious watering in a hot climate, meant that they were grown only by richer landowners. Grapes were principally used for wine-making. The main wine-growing areas were the Delta, the Fayum and the oases of the Western Desert. Many vintages are known by name and vineyards are mentioned in royal records as early as the First Dynasty. The

27. Bottle-shaped basketwork container, which held grapes, from the tomb of Tutankhamun. (Photograph by Egyptian Expedition, Metropolitan Museum of Art, New York. Reproduced by courtesy of the Metropolitan Museum of Art.)

28. Grape harvest and wine pressing. A gardener waters the vines. Theban tomb of Khaemwase, Eighteenth Dynasty.

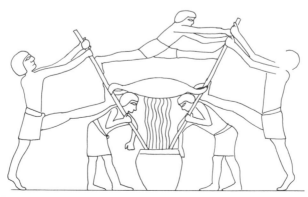

29. Extracting the last drops of juice for wine-making. Tomb of Mereruka at Saqqara, Sixth Dynasty.

vines were grown as stubby bushes or hedges or, more often, in raised beds or troughs from which they were trained to grow up trellises or espaliers. Although most pictures of vines show the black-fruited variety, the range of wines mentioned in texts includes degrees of white as well as sweet and dry types. The darker-skinned grapes were the preferred variety, especially for eating, while other types were grown for specialist wine production.

The process of wine-making was very similar to the traditional European method. The harvested grapes were put into a large vat where they were trodden by a team of chanting workmen. The vat was canopied against the heat and ropes were hung from the rafters

30. Pomegranates from the New Kingdom. (BM 35962-5, author's photograph. By courtesy of the Trustees of the British Museum.)

31. (Below) Pottery, faience and glass vessels from the New Kingdom. (Back row, far left) Tall, papyrus-necked wine jar from a funerary cache of Tutankhamun. (Front row, left) Yellow glass flask in the shape of a pomegranate. (Back row, right) Two narrow-necked bottles of foreign design, of the type used to hold oils.

32. Faience models of fruit: figs, persea fruit and *nabk* berries. Twelfth Dynasty tomb at Lisht. (Metropolitan Museum of Art Excavations 1923-4. Reproduced by courtesy of the Metropolitan Museum of Art.)

33. Banquet guests sniff a mandrake fruit. Theban tomb of Nebamun, Eighteenth Dynasty.

for the treaders to grasp and so steady themselves. The juice ran out through a pipe to be collected in pottery amphorae with tapered bases which were then placed in specially made jar stands. The grape residue of skins, pips and stalks was placed in a sack which was then twisted by means of sticks and manpower to wring out the last drops of juice. The jars were left open or only loosely covered with a pottery cap and the juice allowed to ferment. The warmth of the Egyptian climate was probably enough for fermentation to commence but it is possible that the juice was heated or the jars deliberately placed in the sun to encourage the process. There is some evidence that amphorae were coated inside with a resinous compound to prevent the wine being lost through the porous pottery. The clay used for wine jars was often of a calcareous nature, greenish-grey in colour and less permeable than ordinary domestic wares, but still there must have been considerable loss through evaporation and seepage. For this reason, most Egyptian wines were probably drunk 'young'.

The jars were sealed with plugs of vine leaves or rushes and then the whole top and neck were plastered with a mixture of mud and straw into which seals were pressed to denote the origin and owner-ship of the wine. The jars were commonly inscribed with labels giving details of the type of wine and the year of the vintage. Pliny mentions wines being made from dates, figs and the Egyptian plum (*Cordia myxa*), a stoned fruit similar in shape to a medlar, with a very dry taste.

Another wine was made from pomegranates, a fruit introduced probably via Palestine during the Second Intermediate Period (*c.* 1782-1570 BC). In the tomb of Inenit, a royal architect of the early Eighteenth Dynasty, a text mentions the planting of pomegranate trees. Examples of the fruit have been found in several New Kingdom tombs and its shape was popular for small vases like the yellow glass flask in the Metropolitan Museum, New York (see figure 31). Ancient fruits were smaller than their modern counterparts and were a delicacy.

Another tree prized for its fruit and often included in temple gardens was the persea (*Mimusops laurifolia*). It was thought that the god Thoth wrote the names and titles of kings on the cartouche-shaped leaves of this tree, which was also held sacred to Isis. Persea fruits are found in tombs from as early as the Third Dynasty, when some were placed among the supplies of the Step Pyramid. Models of persea fruit made in wood, stone and faience are displayed at Dokki and were commonly included in burials. The pear-sized fruit is shaped like an almond, has a plum-like stone and a sweetish flavour similar to apple.

Mandrake fruit are often depicted on trays of offerings or represented in jewellery. They are usually shown as yellow with green sepals. The slightly poisonous flesh of the mandrake fruit has a sickly, insipid taste and the stone has high concentrations of several toxins, which have a narcotic effect. It is often shown being held to the nose by guests at a banquet and, as its hallucinatory properties were recognised and it was thought to be an aphrodisiac, the sniffing of the fruit may be the ancient Egyptian equivalent of smoking 'pot'.

The Christ's thorn (*Zizyphus spina-christi*) bears fruit which are known as *nabk* berries. Examples of these cherry-sized fruit have been found in many burials and a dish of fresh *nabk* berries was included in the Saqqara banquet. Offering baskets of small reddish-orange fruit probably represent *nabk,* which the Egyptians called *nebes,* and loaves or cakes made from *nebes* are often listed among funerary and temple supplies.

From all ages come examples of *dom* palm nuts. These shiny, brown fruit, the size and shape of a small capsicum, are still sold in all Egyptian markets. They grow in bunches from the *dom* palm tree,

34. Family scene from Amarna. A dish divided into four sections is filled with fruit: two sorts of figs, pomegranates and *nabk* berries. (Louvre E11624, copyright Musées Nationaux, Paris. Reproduced by courtesy of the Musées Nationaux.)
35. (Below left) Date palm (left) and *dom* palm (right), as depicted in the Theban tomb of Sennedjem, Nineteenth Dynasty.
36. (Below right) Monkey in a *dom* palm. Ostracon from the Fitzwilliam Collection, Cambridge. (Reproduced by permission of the Syndics.)

which differs from the date palm in having a distinctively forked trunk. In ancient times the tree was very widespread but now, apart from areas of the Red Sea coast, it grows no further north in Egypt than

Qena.

It is difficult to imagine how *dom* nuts were eaten as they are so hard and apparently woody. Modern Egyptian practice is to soak from the stone the fibrous, spongy flesh, which is said to have a gingerbread taste, and to eat it raw or to use it, as in ancient times, to make a cake. The hard central stone is a sort of vegetable ivory, used to make beads, rings and other trinkets.

Nuts were uncommon in Egypt. Jars of almonds have been found in some New Kingdom tombs, notably those of Tutankhamun in the Valley of Kings and the architect Kha at Deir el-Medina, but no Egyptian word for almond has yet been identified. Finds of almonds from the workmen's village at Amarna indicate a wider availability than previously thought. Possibly they were imported, as must have been the case with the rare examples of walnuts found in Egyptian sites.

The only nut-like products to be generally available were the tuberous growths on the roots of sedge plants, particularly *Cyperus esculentus*. These ridged, ovoid tubers, which have a taste and texture not unlike coconut, are the size of a peanut and are better known as tigernuts. They are still widely cultivated throughout Africa and are thought to be one of the oldest of Egyptian crops after barley and wheat.

A Nineteenth Dynasty text describing the establishment of the royal palace-town of Pi-Ramesses in the Delta mentions the planting of apple trees in the gardens. Baskets of apples were offered by Ramesses III (Twentieth Dynasty) to the gods but further evidence for the growing of apples in Egypt is very sparse. The Egyptian word translated as apple is *depeh,* which is a loan word derived from Palestinian dialects. This indicates the source of apples, which were probably imported as a luxury fruit rather than being cultivated on a large scale in Egypt. Citrus fruits were not known in Egypt until trees were introduced from more northerly Mediterranean areas during the Graeco-Roman period.

A wide variety of fruit and vegetables was available to and appreciated by the Egyptians. In more elaborate funerary offerings, plant products feature largely. Even in the abbreviated terms of the basic offering formula, the plea for 'all growing things' was popular. The scarcity of evidence for vitamin deficiency diseases such as scurvy or rickets, at least among the middle and upper classes, leads to the reasonable assumption that there were sufficient food plants to maintain a healthy diet.

5
Meat, fish and fowl

The problems associated with keeping food fresh in a hot climate led to an apparent class distinction in the eating of meat. Practically speaking, the lower a person's class, the smaller the animal he was likely to eat. Only a wealthy man could afford to slaughter an animal the size of an ox. Cattle were the most highly prized of all domestic animals. The most easily recognised joint of meat presented at tomb or temple was the haunch or leg of beef. In the Pyramid Texts, this joint figures largely as the most prestigious offering and its shape was even recognised in the sky as the Egyptian name for the constellation Ursa Major was the Haunch. It is unlikely that the lowliest peasant ever had the opportunity to taste beef or even pork, mutton or goat meat.

The basic animal protein sources for most Egyptians were fish and wildfowl. This dependence on low-fat meats meant that obesity was not a substantial problem for the greater part of the population. However, it was common for a well-to-do man to have himself portrayed with rolls of fat about his midriff. This does not mean that all wealthy men were overweight, though doubtless some were, but by this convention a man's prosperity and success were indicated.

There is evidence of taboos associated with different meats, but these appear to have been more often social than religious and, if religious, then confined to a specific region or group of people. The eating of pork is quoted by many sources as having been forbidden to the Egyptians. Herodotus details the festivities held in memory of Horus' victory over Seth, to whom the pig was sacred. It was, he said, the only time of the year when people ate pork and those families who could not afford a pig would eat loaves made in the shape of the animal. At the Middle Kingdom town of Kahun and the Eighteenth Dynasty workmen's village at Amarna, large quantities of pig bones have been found, indicating that pork played a significant role in the diet of the working-class Egyptian.

There are similar reports of a taboo on fish, which may have applied to the priesthood and, by reason of his position as high priest of all cults, to the king. Scenes of fishermen at work and presentations of fish appear in the tombs of high-ranking court officials, proving that the taboo, if it existed, was by no means universal within the nobility. The profession of fisherman was despised by all classes, although, in itself, the fish was considered to be a lucky charm. A fish amulet tied into the youthful side-lock was thought to protect

37. Stela of Sirenenutet, Twelfth Dynasty, showing an offering table laden with food including joints of meat: haunch, ribs and head. (BM EA585, author's photograph. By courtesy of the Trustees of the British Museum.)

a child from drowning.

Modern analyses of fish bones from Predynastic sites such as Hierakonpolis are adding new information about diet and it is possible to identify some fish species which flourished in the Nile in Dynastic times from the representations of them shown in waterside scenes. But not all are immediately recognisable as the river no longer supports such a varied fish population. In the Eighteenth Dynasty Deir el-Bahri reliefs of Queen Hatshepsut's Punt expedition, it is possible to identify marine species including a turtle, a lobster and an octopus or squid. It is unlikely that the inhabitants of the Nile Valley relied to any extent on sea fish because of the difficulties involved in transporting and delivering a catch in an edible condition. The recording of Red Sea species, therefore, is not necessarily an indication that these were regularly caught for food.

The simplest, and probably the oldest, means of catching fish was to drive them into the shallows where a stake and net enclosure trapped them. The fishermen then scooped them out by hand or net, or speared them. Bottle-shaped basketwork traps, weighted with stones and marked by floats, were also set in the water at the river's edge. Small rafts made of reed bundles were paddled into deeper water where wooden-framed scoop nets could be used. The same boats were used to take out long seine nets which were then hauled in by men on shore. Pairs of larger boats, rowed by teams of oarsmen, fished with trawl nets stretched between them. Multi-hooked lines, resembling mackerel lines, were used by the individual fisherman, who held a club ready to kill the fish as they were landed.

The catch was collected in sacks or rushwork bags or the fish were threaded on to strings and then tied in bundles to a pole. Some were delivered at once to the market. Much of the catch was cleaned, gutted and slabbed, that is, split open down the backbone and flatten-

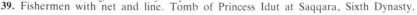

38. Offerings of eggs, cucumbers, fish, pigeons and two sealed jars of honey. Theban tomb of Menna, Eighteenth Dynasty.
39. Fishermen with net and line. Tomb of Princess Idut at Saqqara, Sixth Dynasty.

40. Dish of sun-dried fish. (BM 36191, author's photograph. By courtesy of the Trustees of the British Museum.)

ed, either on the boat or as soon as it reached the riverbank. The prepared fish were allowed to hang in the sun from wooden frames or from the boat's rigging to dry. In modern Middle Eastern countries, fish is still prepared in this way and is occasionally buried in hot sand or mud to mature for a few days. Fires are not shown in connection with the slabbing of fish but it is quite likely that fish were smoked as well as dried.

Fish were also salted or pickled in oil and, in later times, great quantities of preserved fish were exported from Egypt. In some scenes of fish preparation, removal of the roes is shown. The dried and salted roe of the grey mullet, known as *batarekh,* is considered a great delicacy in modern Egypt and is reputed to be a recipe as old as the pharaohs. In one of the rare market scenes, close to sellers of fish, a woman is seen offering for sale round white objects, which may be the ancient equivalent of *qras samak,* a sort of fishcake which has been prepared throughout the Middle East for centuries (see figure 6).

A multitude of bird species inhabited the reedbeds along the Nile. Ducks, geese, finches, egrets, storks and cranes were hunted for food and for sport. The number of species found in the Nile Valley was far greater in Dynastic times than today. For example, the red-breasted goose so clearly depicted in the Fourth Dynasty tomb of Itet at Meydum is no longer found in Egypt, even at the southernmost extent of its range. A favourite pastime of the nobility was to spend a pleasant afternoon in the company of the family, hunting wildfowl with throwing sticks or bow and arrows.

The profession of wildfowler was considered degrading despite being essential to the peasant food supply. Birds were speared, shot with bow and arrow or, on a larger scale, caught in spring traps or

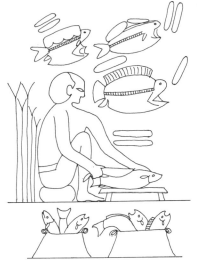

41. Preparation of fish. The fish are 'slabbed' and the roes are removed. Tomb of Princess Idut at Saqqara, Sixth Dynasty.

42. Force-feeding geese. The man on the right prepares pellets of bread sweetened with dried fruit and moistened with oil or wine. Tomb of Kagemni at Saqqara, Sixth Dynasty.

large draw nets. Some may have been captured alive then fattened for the table like the flock of cranes shown in the Old Kingdom tomb of Ptah-hotep at Saqqara. Others were apparently force-fed with bread or a sweetened mash so perhaps the Egyptians had a taste for *pâté de foie gras.*

Ducks and geese were kept in poultry pens and yards where they were fed on grain. The Egyptians had to rely on ducks and geese for eggs as domestic fowl were not introduced into the country in

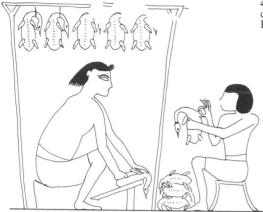

43. Plucking and cleaning ducks. Theban tomb of Nakht, Eighteenth Dynasty.

any numbers until Roman times. Other birds, including pigeons and, apparently, pelicans, as seen in the Eighteenth Dynasty tomb of the scribe Horemheb, were also kept as egg-layers. Eggs for offerings are shown in bowls layered between fresh green leaves, which helped to keep them cool.

Birds were prepared for the table in much the same way as in modern practice. They were plucked, drawn and hung. Herodotus wrote that some small birds were preserved by being dried, salted or pickled and men are frequently shown in scenes of poultry preparation packing ducks into large jars which presumably contained oil or brine (see figure 48). A roast goose was a very desirable dish for special occasions such as religious festivals and was the equivalent of the modern Christmas turkey. The Greeks and Romans found it hard to understand that the Egyptians should consider eating geese when the birds were so sacred. The goose was emblematic of the national god Amun-Re of Thebes.

Smaller birds shown being eaten whole, as in banqueting scenes from Amarna, could have been pigeons or quail. Most villages and larger estates would have had their own dovecotes and quail were

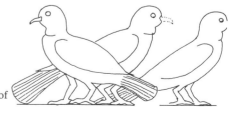

44. Domestic pigeons or doves. Tomb of Ti at Saqqara, Sixth Dynasty.

45. Prepared duck or pigeon. The body has been slit along its length and pressed flat. From Deir el-Medina, Eighteenth Dynasty. (Louvre E14551, copyright Musées Nationaux, Paris. Reproduced by courtesy of the Musées Nationaux.)

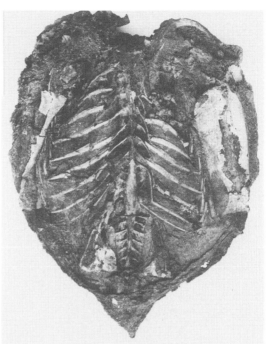

caught as they rested in Egypt during their annual migration. The ancient way of preparing pigeons was much the same as that used in modern Egypt, where they are still considered a delicacy. The birds were split in half, flattened and grilled. The Saqqara banquet included a cooked quail presented with its head tucked under a wing, and a stew of small birds which Emery identified as pigeons.

Most scenes of butchery deal with the preparation of cattle carcases, always oxen (see figures 16 and 49). It seems that cows were not killed for their meat, or at least not for religious offerings, but were kept for breeding and for milk. The bound oxen were slaughtered by having their throats cut and the blood, which was saved, may have been used to make a kind of sausage or black pudding. The carcase was cut into joints such as the haunch, a rack of ribs, the head and a juicy-looking steak with a bone passing through it. In butchery scenes, pieces of meat are often shown being hung up on lines or racks. Some may have been allowed to dry in the sun to make a kind of biltong. Offal was also treated in this way, the liver and heart being favoured. Meat dishes in the Saqqara banquet consisted of a pair of cooked kidneys, probably from a sheep, goat or pig, and two dishes including beef ribs.

46. Butcher's shop with joints of meat hanging on lines. Section through a model from the tomb of Meket-Re, Eleventh Dynasty. (After Winlock.)

Although the preferred methods of cooking meat were roasting or grilling, it is clear from some tomb reliefs that lesser cuts were braised or stewed. The bones and scraps were boiled and reduced for stock or soup as indicated by the so-called Cannibal Hymn from the Pyramid Texts: 'Their spirits are in the King's possession / As the broth of the gods, / Which is cooked for the King out of their bones.' The skin, hooves and gristle were used to make glue and the fat and

47. Wild game for the nobleman's table. Servants bring hares and an antelope or gazelle. Theban tomb of User, Eighteenth Dynasty. (After Davies.)

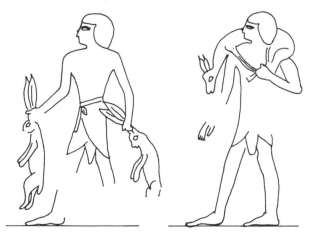

suet were kept for cooking. Possibly bread and dripping were one of the perks of being a servant in a rich man's kitchen.

The diet of the nobleman could be supplemented by wild game caught on hunting expeditions. Several species of antelope and gazelle, wild sheep and goats and smaller game like desert hares feature in hunting scenes, particularly from the Old Kingdom. They were hunted with spear or bow or, on occasion, captured alive by means of a lasso or bolas. Live animals were fattened in animal pens and may have been force-fed. Scenes which apparently illustrate this practice involve addax and oryx but, as the force-feeding of ruminants is not likely to have been successful, it is possible that such scenes represent veterinary treatment of the beasts.

The most prestigious of game, wild cattle, were reserved for the king's sport. Herds of these beasts were still to be found in Egypt at least until the Twentieth Dynasty, when Ramesses III had a magnificent representation of the hunt carved into the first pylon of his Medinet Habu temple. The Eighteenth Dynasty king Amenophis III issued a commemorative scarab recording his single-handed killing of more than a hundred animals from one herd. Reading between the lines, it seems that the cattle were corralled by his followers so the hunt was more a slaughter of helpless beasts. It seems very extravagant to kill that number of animals at one time because of the problems associated with disposing of large amounts of fresh meat. Even the temples could not have accepted that number of carcases, especially as they were not killed in the prescribed manner in the temple abattoirs, overseen by priests.

A classic Egyptian dish which is said to have its origins in the pharaonic age is *ferique,* a stew made with a chicken, a calf's foot, whole grain and eggs in their shells. If for chicken we read duck, all the ingredients were available to the ancients. It would be tempting to see a link between the word pharaoh and the name of the dish but this is more precisely derived from the Arabic word *ferakh* meaning chicken.

The preparation of meat for the table and the cooking techniques employed were much the same for whatever animal, sheep, pig or ox, that was to be eaten. There is no evidence of elaborate sauces or of plated meals consisting of meat and two vegetables. The meat was served with various sorts of bread and this would have been true of the fish and fowl eaten by the peasant or the good roast beef on the nobleman's table.

6
The condiment shelf

The most basic of diets may be enlivened and varied by the careful use of condiments. Certain of these, such as salt, oil and vinegar, are also essential to some common methods of food preservation.

The remains of vinegar, whether from the brewer's or the vintner's vats, would be indistinguishable from the residues of beer or wine, so it is not known for certain that the Egyptians used vinegar. However, given the prevalence of beer and wines and their tendency to go sour in hot climates, it is unlikely that the Egyptians never discovered the use of vinegar in flavouring and preserving food.

Salt was probably the oldest and most useful condiment available to all classes, but the methods used by the Egyptians to extract a pure form for table use are unknown. It is assumed that a certain amount was obtained from pans on the Mediterranean and Red Sea coasts and from naturally occurring salt deposits, particularly in the Western Desert and the oases. Other salt pans must have been in use but have not been identified. Samples of salt relatively free from the major impurities of carbonates and sulphates have been found at Gebelein dating from the Sixth Dynasty.

Several different sorts of salt are named in offering lists from Old and New Kingdom tombs, including northern and red salt. The 'Eloquent Peasant', in the Twelfth Dynasty story of that name, included salt among the products he was taking to market since salt was an acceptable commodity for barter. Salt gatherers were employed by the temples and in the Twentieth Dynasty some were granted special status by Ramesses III. Herodotus mentioned the mining of purple salt in Libya.

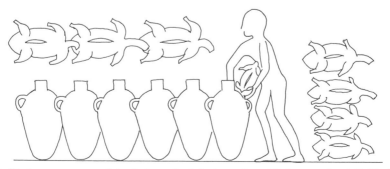

48. Ducks are preserved by being salted in large jars. Theban tomb of Rekhmire, Eighteenth Dynasty.

49. Stela showing brewing, baking, butchery and presentation of animals. The goatherd carries a bowl which may have held milk or cheeses. (BM 1372, reproduced by courtesy of the Trustees of the British Museum.)

Most importantly, salt was used for curing and preserving fish and meat. Large quantities of preserved fish, presumably dried and salted, were exported from Egypt. An act of hospitality still common in the Middle East, and undoubtedly of ancient origin, is the offering of bread sprinkled with salt. This symbolic meal seals a guest-friendship and its acceptance by a visitor is a tacit promise to respect the host's household. In modern Egypt, the simplest of snack meals or appetisers is bread served with *dukkah,* a condiment mix. The ingredients may

50. Asiatic traders unloading a cargo of oils. The merchant in his fringed gown offers a sealed jar of oil for valuation. Theban tomb of Qenamun, Eighteenth Dynasty. (After Davies.)

51. An olive branch offered to Aten. From an Amarnan relief now in New York.

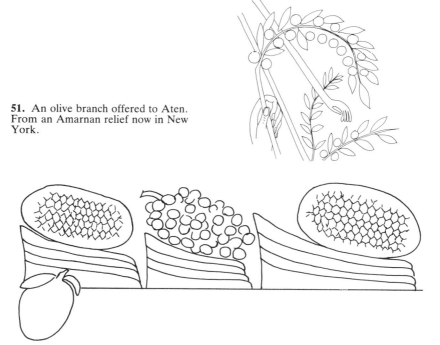

52. Sweet offerings; fruit, honeycombs and honey cakes. Theban tomb of Userhat, Eighteenth Dynasty.

include sesame, coriander and cumin seed, ground nuts, dried herbs, salt and pepper. The simplest and cheapest form of *dukkah* is that sold in paper packets in the market place: a mix of salt with a little pepper and dried mint.

Natron, a naturally occurring crystalline mixture of sodium carbonate (washing soda) and sodium bicarbonate (baking soda) with variable amounts of sodium chloride (table salt) and sodium sulphate, was used extensively in the preparation of bodies for mummification. It has a strong degreasing and dehydrating action and dissolves fatty tissue. In the temple, natron was very important in purification rituals. There is little evidence for the use of natron in cookery but its inclusion among food rations provided for the workmen of Deir el-Medina may indicate its domestic use, possibly for curing meats.

Alum is known to have been mined in the Kharga Oasis in the Libyan desert from ancient times but no word for this compound has yet been definitely identified. It was probably mostly used as a mordant or fixing agent in dyeing but, as in some eastern countries today, it could be used to curdle milk without souring for making cheese.

Most village dwellers could have had access to a supply of goat's or sheep's milk. As fresh milk would not keep long in Egypt's heat, some may have been cultured into a product like yoghurt. Jars found with the Saqqara banquet are thought to have contained some sort of cultured milk or curd cheese.

A simple cheese called *labna* is made in modern Egypt by straining salted yoghurt to a creamy consistency. It may be served for breakfast spread on bread, or mixed with oil and fresh herbs. Balls of the thickest *labna* are preserved in oil. A firmer cheese, *gebna,* is made from pressed, salted curds and may be kept for two or three days to dry and harden. Both *labna* and *gebna* could have been produced by the ancient Egyptians. Two jars from the tomb of Hor-aha (First Dynasty) yielded fatty residues which have been identified as the remains of cheese.

It is almost impossible to assign any of the Egyptian words for milk products to particular foodstuffs. Neither cream nor butter would have kept well but clarified butter, *samna* in Arabic, is still very common. It is made by solidifying the liquid strained off from butter that has been heated until it froths. Sometimes *samna* is mixed with aromatic spices like fenugreek or caraway and it will keep for a long time in a cool place. The elimination of salt and water lessen the tendency of butter to burn and discolour.

For the poorer household, the most useful cooking fat would be that obtained from rendering a sheep's tail. In Egypt today this fat is called *alya*. Since pigs were common, lard could have been used in cooking, as could suet. Among the temple offerings of Ramesses III was listed 'white fat for cakes', which may be identified as one of these rendered fats. Poorer households used duck or goose grease in large quantities both for cooking and as bases for cosmetics.

The oldest royal food list, from the Sixth Dynasty Pyramid of Unas, includes five kinds of oil. Oil was an important food item as shown by its inclusion in the daily rations issued to royal servants like the King's Messenger and Standard Bearer from the reign of Seti I. He received, as his wages: '. . . good bread, ox flesh, wine, sweet oil, olive oil(?), fat, honey, figs, fish and vegetables every day'.

One of the most popular oil-bearing plants in Egypt was the *hegelig* tree, also known as Egyptian balsam (*Balanites aegyptiaca*). Examples of the fig-shaped fruit have been found in tombs of all periods including the Step Pyramid. They commonly show a small hole bored into the flesh through which the oil-bearing seed was extracted. The sweetly scented oil was used for cooking and as a base for perfumes.

Another very popular oil, probably the 'sweet oil' in the Standard Bearer's list, was that extracted from the seeds of the *ben* tree (*Moringa peregrina*). The tree is almost leafless and bears its edible nuts in pods. The Egyptians called the tree, and the oil obtained from its seeds, *bak*, and the oil is commonly named in the offering lists of all periods. The tree is now very scarce in Egypt.

Oils which are now out of favour for culinary use were extracted from a variety of seeds including lettuce and radish, castor oil and linseed. The latter two oils may have been used predominantly for lighting while linseed oil is traditionally used in Egyptian cookery, particularly for flavouring *ful medames*. Castor oil, though highly distasteful to Western palates, is still used around the Middle East as a cooking oil.

Floral tributes in burials include safflowers, so oil may have been extracted from their seed, but most probably the commonest cooking oil was that obtained from sesame seed. There is little direct evidence for the ancient production of sesame oil but the plant was certainly grown in Egypt from at least the Eighteenth Dynasty, and quantities of the oil were imported from Palestine. Despite the similarity between the Arabic *semsem* (sesame) and the Egyptian plant name *shemshemet,* it is thought that they do not refer to the same plant since the Egyptians called the oil *neheh.*

There is a possible reference in the Old Kingdom Pyramid Texts to sacred olive trees grown at El-Matariya and in the Eighteenth Dynasty Akhenaten was shown presenting an olive branch with leaves and fruit to Aten. Olive trees were grown in Egypt, as shown by the leaves in funerary wreaths from Theban tombs and settlement sites

53. Figs, like dates, were important sweeteners, used in purée form in baking. (BM 5368, reproduced by courtesy of the Trustees of the British Museum.)

like Amarna. Possibly small amounts of oil were produced but represented a minor contribution to Egypt's total oil requirement. Even as late as the reign of Ptolemy II, when comprehensive laws governing oil production, distribution and sale were published, olive oil was not mentioned. Either the Egyptian crop was not sufficient or the quality of the fruit not suitable for pressing.

Nearly thirty types of oil are known by name from Egyptian sources. Some may represent the products of particular regions, including imported oils, and others may be blends or oils flavoured with aromatics or herbs. Not all the oils would have been used for cooking and many have yet to be identified. Even the remains in labelled jars are difficult to analyse.

The sweet product valued above all others was honey. From oldest times, the bee has been a symbol of Lower Egypt, where the extensive pasture-lands and beds of flowering reeds provided an ideal environment for apiculture. The honey was stored in different-shaped jars, possibly according to quality, and the lids were sealed with wax (see figure 38). In the scene of tax deliveries in the Theban tomb of the vizier Rekhmire (Eighteenth Dynasty), honey is shown being brought by many district representatives. Whole honeycombs are occasionally shown among food offerings, as in the Nineteenth Dynasty

54. Woman and child beneath a carob tree.
Theban tomb of Nakht, Eighteenth Dynasty.
The hieroglyph for 'sweet' is shown (top
right) for comparison with the pods on the
tree.

55. (Below) The first fruits of the harvest, all
draped with leafy produce, probably herbs,
are presented to the landowner. Theban
tomb of Djeserkeresonb, Eighteenth Dynasty. (After Davies.)

56. Conical pot-baked loaf with coating of seeds. (By permission of Museum of Fine Arts, Boston.)
57. Model showing grinding grain, kneading dough and baking in a makeshift oven made of stone slabs. (BM 55730, reproduced by courtesy of the Trustees of the British Museum.)

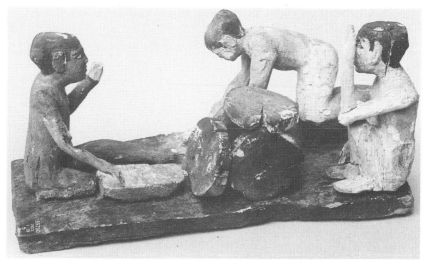

tomb of Userhat, a priest during the reign of Seti I.

The less well-off would have used fruit, particularly dates and figs, as sweeteners. Sauces could be sweetened with fruit purée or a concentrated fruit juice like that pomegranate syrup which is still widely used in Middle Eastern cookery. Carob, the powdered pods of the St John's locust (*Ceratonia siliqua*), was also known to the Egyptians. Pods and seeds have been found at Kahun and Deir el-Medina. The word *nedjem,* which refers to a tree and its fruit, is thought to represent carob. The hieroglyphic symbol for 'sweet' is derived from a carob bean pod as carob has a high sugar content.

Herbs were grown in garden plots as well as being picked from the wild. Parsley (the flat-leafed kind) and coriander were predominant, both being used to flavour meat. Coriander seed has been found in quantity in tombs of all periods. The celery included in Tutankhamun's funeral bouquet had stems no thicker than those of parsley: ancient celery was more like a herb for flavouring than a vegetable. Of the two terms translated as 'desert parsley' and 'mountain parsley', the latter may represent celery.

Rosemary grows naturally in Egypt and is assumed to have been available in ancient times, though recorded finds of rosemary may be spurious. Leaves of mint and sage have been found from later periods but other herbs, like dill, chervil and fennel, may be represented among the list of unattributed plant names.

A basketful of cumin seed was included in the burial of the architect Kha. Whole seeds were sprinkled on bread dough before baking and the ground spice was probably used to flavour meat. In the absence of peppercorns, which were not imported from India until Graeco-Roman times, cumin was probably the most important of aromatic seasonings.

Fenugreek, with its distinctive curry smell, has been found at Maadi, south of Cairo, dating from about 3000 BC. Mustard of the black-seeded variety has been found in New Kingdom tombs and, as poppies were grown for their flowers and for medicinal purposes, their seed would have been available for cookery.

A spice called *ty-sheps* was considered very important, as might be seen from its name, which means 'indeed noble'. It was imported in quantity though the place of origin is uncertain. It was probably traded in Syria, which was the nearest point to Egypt on the route of the spice caravans from the Far East. As *ty-sheps* was offered in bundles it has tentatively been identified as cinnamon bark.

Enough condiments were available even to the poorest peasants to make Egyptian cuisine varied and appetising. The range of herbs and spices was similar to that used in modern Arab cookery.

7
The kitchen

There are many surviving representations of Egyptian kitchens, notably in the Sixth Dynasty tomb of Ti at Saqqara, the tomb models of Meket-Re from the Eleventh Dynasty and the Twentieth Dynasty tomb of Ramesses III. From these it seems that, throughout the Dynastic age, the standard equipment of the Egyptian kitchen, and the basic cooking techniques employed in it, changed very little.

Peasant workmen would cook their food out of doors. A duck was toasted over a fire on a stick threaded through the neck and body cavity, while bread baked in the ashes. A simple oven could be constructed from limestone slabs, the roof becoming a bakestone (see figure 57).

Most household cooking was done in the open air, or in a courtyard partly roofed with matting or palm thatch, to allow the escape of smoke. In the workmen's village at Amarna some kitchens were placed on an upper floor or the roof, so preventing cooking smells from invading the living quarters. A hearth might have a back wall against which a sizable heap of embers could be piled. Into this were placed bread moulds or pots for slow cooking (see figure 13). Larger pots with loop handles or heavy rims were suspended by cords above the fire.

The domestic cooking fire was laid in a dished pottery 'hearth', often set into the floor (see figure 64). A bow drill twisting a rod in the hollow of a base block generated enough heat to ignite straw, which was then used to light the fire. The cook encouraged the flames with a papyrus or palm leaf fan while protecting his face from the heat with his raised forearm. Straw, palm leaves and animal dung were used for fuel as well as small branches of acacia and tamarisk, some wood being first made into charcoal.

The usual domestic stove was cylindrical and of clay, with an arched stoke-hole, a shape so familiar that it was used as the hieroglyph for the consonant G. The butchery model from Meket-Re's tomb includes a stove with a crenellated top which allowed smoke to escape around the edges of a pan resting on it. Several cooking pot shapes may be identified from relief and painting. 'Frying pans' were wok-shaped with lug or loop handles. Pots for braising, or preparing such dishes as porridge, curved inwards at the top to reduce loss through evaporation. Large stew pans, shown full of joints of meat, had straight sides and flat bases. In ordinary kitchens of all periods, cooking pots were made of unglazed Nile clay, sometimes

58. Model house with food offerings laid out in the courtyard. An unroofed area to the left could represent the kitchen. A staircase leads to a roof space which could also be used for cooking. (BM 32610, author's photograph. By courtesy of the Trustees of the British Museum.)

59. Wooden models of stoves from Meket-Re's tomb, Eleventh Dynasty: (a) portable box oven/stove with cooking pot; (b) portable brazier with crenellated top and stew pan in place; (c) cylindrical stove with shallow frying pan. (After Winlock.)

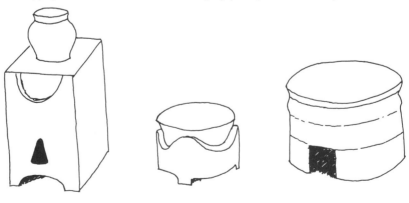

a   b   c

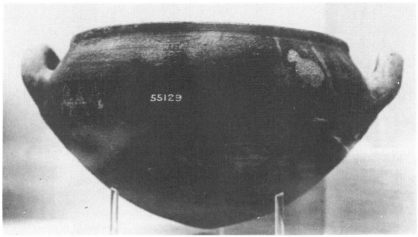

60. Pottery cooking bowl with loop handles. (BM 55129, author's photograph. By courtesy of the Trustees of the British Museum.)

with a burnished slip coating. Wealthier households might use copper vessels or, in later periods, bronze.

Domed bake-ovens were commonly of moulded clay with a flat baking floor under which the fire was stoked. Hot air and smoke circulated into the oven through a gap to one side. Box ovens were used for baking batches of moulded bread. One such oven, packed with bread moulds, was found at Amarna in 1986. Smaller box ovens were like kitchen ranges with holes in the top into which cooking pans would fit.

Knives were of copper or bronze though peasant housewives may have made do with flint. Double-edged blades had straight handles while the handles of those with one cutting edge were curved. Some large butchers' knives were serrated to cut through tendons and cartilage. The turned-up point of a single-edged knife, sometimes with a decorated tip, served two purposes. It prevented the knife snagging and spoiling skins intended for leather and it enabled the cook to hold the point while chopping or slicing.

The simplest cooking utensil was a long stick or pair of sticks used to extract cooked items from a pan or loaves from an oven. Removing bread from a large bake-oven was a potentially hazardous business as indicated by this extract from a Nineteenth Dynasty schoolboy text: 'When the baker comes to bake and lays the bread on the fire, his head is inside the oven, and his son holds on tightly to his feet. Should it happen that he slips from his son's hand, he will fall into the blaze.'

61. (Above left) Decorated tip of a bronze butcher's knife from Kerma, Second Intermediate Period. (By permission of Museum of Fine Arts, Boston, 20.1799.)
62. (Above right) Segmented bowl carved from a single piece of wood, used to serve fruit. (See also figure 34.)
63. Model table service of limestone, Fifth or Sixth Dynasty. (Metropolitan Museum of Art. Rogers Funds 1911, 11.150.2. Reproduced by courtesy of the Metropolitan Museum of Art.

Wooden spoons and spatulas were used for stirring, turning and sampling food during cooking (see figure 14). Some larger spoons and ladles were of metal and pierced 'skimmers' are known. A stone pestle and mortar were included in the *batterie* of the Egyptian cook, for grinding spices and nuts and as a mixing bowl.

Food, even for the gods, was served on rushwork mats. Wooden bowls, some divided into several sections, others with sliding lids, were used to store and serve fruit. For table use, pottery plates, bowls and cups were found in all households. The better-off could afford decorative wares of faience and stone. The Theban burial of three Syrian wives of Tuthmosis III (mid Eighteenth Dynasty) included fine dishes and beakers of gold and silver.

Most Egyptian storage vessels, like wine amphorae and meat jars, had rounded bases so they were kept in ring stands or set into the

64. Kitchen scenes from Amarna. A servant tends a fire in a pottery hearth. Wine amphorae and other storage jars are seen in pantries. (By permission of Museum of Fine Arts, Boston, 63.962.)

65. A kitchen in the workmen's village at Amarna, excavated by the Egypt Exploration Society, 1921. The cylindrical oven and quern emplacement are seen *in situ*. The latter still bears traces of whitewash. (By courtesy of the Committee of the Egypt Exploration Society.)

floor (see figure 31). Wine jars represented at banquets are shown in racks, decorated with floral garlands. Occasionally they are provided with siphons or straws so that wine could be taken from the jars without disturbing the inevitable sediment. Wines were also mixed and spiced to taste. When wine or beer was poured from a smaller jar it was usually passed through a drink strainer of pierced metal.

Throughout the Dynastic age, basketwork containers were used by all classes for storing and transporting foodstuffs. In Predynastic times, communal grain stores were simply matting- or basket-lined pits, while rushwork sacks or jars were used for domestic storage. Larger estates, from the Old Kingdom onwards, had brick-built corn bunkers with roof-top access for filling. Mud-brick silos shaped like beehives were also used for large quantities of grain and were imitated in pottery as household bins.

Dry goods were stored and transported in baskets, sacks or jars. More precious goods, such as spices, salt and natron, were kept in small leather or linen bags with drawstring tops, while oils and fats might be kept in stoneware jars.

The insecticidal properties of ash were utilised in disinfecting areas associated with grain. In Predynastic sites in the Fayum, granary pits have been found to contain wood ash mixed with the grain. This was either intended to deter insect attack or was the result of a deliberate burning to clean out the pit. During the 1986 season of the Egypt Exploration Society's work at Amarna, quern emplacements were found with layers of ash over the working surface. This was apparently a means of sterilising the area. Walls around such emplacements and other food preparation areas such as butchers' slabs were often whitewashed. Natron, which contains high proportions of washing soda, could have been used as a household cleanser.

Vermin presented problems for the Egyptian housewife of all eras. Mouse and rat holes are found at most settlement sites and pottery rat traps were in use during the Twelfth Dynasty at Kahun. Gerbils also proliferated. The popularity of the domestic cat must have been, in some part, due to its mousing instincts.

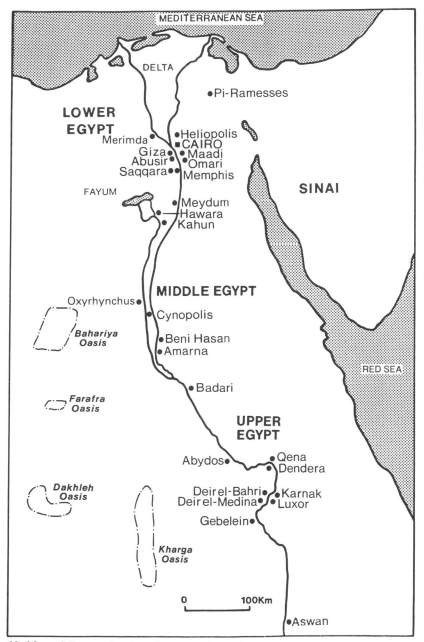

66. Map of Egypt, showing places mentioned in the text.

8
Glossary

Alya: rendered fat from a sheep's tail.

Barm: liquid yeast skimmed from the surface of a fermented liquor such as beer.

Batarekh: pressed, dried and salted roe of the grey mullet.

Bedoukhia: large, dark green water-melon.

Bouza: a potent beer made in the Sudan.

Dom: palm tree bearing hard, shiny, brown nuts.

Dukkah: a mixture of coarsely ground nuts, spices, dried herbs and salt, sprinkled over bread and eaten as a snack or appetiser.

Eish shami: Arab bread, like pitta bread, sometimes made with a central depression into which an egg is cracked before baking.

Emmer: primitive form of wheat.

Felafel: fried rissoles of mashed beans or chick-peas with onion, garlic, cumin and fresh coriander.

Ferique: a stew made with a chicken, a calf's foot, eggs in their shells and whole-grain wheat.

Ful medames: national Egyptian dish of stewed brown beans served with garlic, onion, oil and cumin.

Gebna beida: firm white cheese made from pressed, salted curds.

Hummus: puréed chick-peas with sesame oil.

Jujube: see *Nabk*.

Labna: soft cream cheese made by straining salted yoghurt through a cloth.

Lupine: bitter-tasting bean of the lupin family.

Magur: large metal bread-mixing vessel.

Malt: barley grains that have been allowed to sprout before being dried in hot air.

Meloukhia: plant of the hemp family, picked like spinach and used to make a glutinous soup of the same name.

Mezze: a small meal in the form of snacks, *hors d'oeuvres* or side dishes, often served with drinks.

Nabk: orange-red, cherry-sized fruit of the Christ's thorn tree.

Natron: naturally occurring crystalline mixture of sodium carbonate and sodium bicarbonate with varying degrees of impurity in the form of sodium chloride and sodium sulphate.

Pancheon: traditional English bread-mixing crock, shaped like a flaring flower pot, glazed on the inner surface only.

Parch: to dry out dampened grain, in the sun or by light roasting, in order to facilitate milling.

Qras samak: fishcakes made with pounded fish, cracked wheat, fresh coriander and seasoning.

Samna: clarified butter or butter oil, made by straining off impurities, including salt, from melted butter.

Ta'amia: see *Felafel.*

Temper (in baking): to create a temporary non-stick surface in earthenware bread moulds by greasing and heating several times.

Tirmiss: see *Lupine.*

9
Museums to visit

United Kingdom
British Museum, Great Russell Street, London WC1B 3DG. Telephone: 01-636 1555.

Manchester Museum, University of Manchester, Oxford Road, Manchester M13 9PL. Telephone: 061-273 3333.

Petrie Museum of Egyptian Archaeology, University College London, Gower Street, London WC1E 6BT. Telephone: 01-387 7050 extension 2884.

Egypt
Egyptian Antiquities Museum, Tahrir Square, Cairo.

Museum of Ancient Agriculture, El Dokki, Giza, Cairo.

France
Musée du Louvre, Palais du Louvre, 75003 Paris.

Italy
Museo Egizio, Palazzo dell' Accademia della Scienze, Via Accademia della Scienze 6, Turin.

United States of America
Brooklyn Museum, 188 Eastern Parkway, Brooklyn, New York 11238.

Metropolitan Museum of Art, 5th Avenue at 82nd Street, New York 10028.

Museum of Fine Arts, Huntington Avenue, Boston, Massachusetts 02115.

10
Further reading

Abdennour, S. *Egyptian Cooking: A Practical Guide.* The American University in Cairo Press, 1984.

Aldred, C. *Akhenaten and Nefertiti.* Thames and Hudson, 1973.

Berriedale-Johnson, M. *The British Museum Cookbook.* British Museum Publications, 1987.

The Daily Life of the Ancient Egyptians. A guide to some of the every-day artefacts on display at the Metropolitan Museum of Art, New York. Not dated.

Darby, W. *et al. Food: The Gift of Osiris* (two volumes). Academic Press, London, New York and San Francisco, 1977.

Egypt's Golden Age: The Art of Living in the New Kingdom. An exhibition catalogue produced by the Museum of Fine Arts, Boston, 1982.

Emery, W. B. *A Funerary Repast in an Egyptian Tomb of the Archaic Period.* Leiden, 1962.

Germer, R. *Flora des Pharaonischen Ägypten.* Mainz, 1980.

Roden, C. *A New Book of Middle Eastern Food.* Penguin, 1986.

Stead, M. *Egyptian Life.* British Museum Publications, 1986.

PENGUIN RE

THE PENGUIN DICTIONARY OF
INFORMATION TECHNOLOGY

Tony Gunton is an independent consultant and author, specializing in the management implications of information technology. Since graduating from Cambridge University with a degree in modern languages he has spent over twenty years in the information-technology industry. He has operated in a variety of roles, including product development, project and line management and, most recently, consultancy and sponsored research. He was one of the founders of Butler, Cox & Partners Ltd, a UK-based management consulting firm specializing in information technology that has established a very high reputation worldwide. He is author of *End User Focus, Infrastructure: Building a Framework for Corporate Information Handling* and *Inside Information Technology: A Guide to the Management Issues* and editor of the Prentice–Hall Business Information Technology series.